Come Hell
or High Water

Blooming Twig Books
New York / Tulsa

"High energy, enthusiastic, knowledgeable
and easy to understand..."

- Tom Stirewalt, Ancillary Computers

"Marvin LeBlanc has a sense of humor but understands
the importance of changing peoples' lives!"

- Deanna Faris, *CopyTalk.com*

"It's never too late to revitalize your career
and become *significant*. Thanks, Marvin,
I owe you more than you'll ever know."

- Mike Coleman, State Farm Insurance

"If everyone took heed of Marvin LeBlanc's words,
we would live in a much better and happier place.
Nothing's impossible if you want it bad enough!"

- Benjamin Cairns, Crain Communications

"It is always interesting, to say the least, to see what
some of our fellow agents have been through and how
they have handled the stress and challenges that go hand
in hand with such a devastating natural occurrence."

- Rob Mabe, State Farm Insurance

"I love the Adversity Expert that Marvin is, and *then* some!"

- Kathleen Wilkin, Safeguard Business Systems

All photographs by Joshua Lee
www.joshualeestudio.com

Published by:
Blooming Twig Books
New York / Tulsa
www.bloomingtwig.com

For bulk purchases, please contact Blooming Twig Books:
320 S. Boston, Suite 1026 / Tulsa, OK 74103
Tel: 1-866-389-1482 / Fax: 1-866-298-7260

ISBN 978-1-933918-89-1

First Edition, First Printing

Dedicated to

Mary "Doosie" Duplessis,
a grandmother's grandmother.
She embodied the ability to provide
firmness and structure with the
perfect mix of love and laughter.

Joyce LeBlanc, my mother.
Known to thousands as "Aunt Joyce."
Her selfless efforts grew a city of leaders
and a son who was privileged to be in her
front seat on the ride of a lifetime.

The C.Y.O Kids.
All of you know who you are, because you all
grew up at my house. You've danced with me,
teased me, held me, cried with me, laughed with
me, played every sport with me and spanked
me. In a word, you molded and inspired
me. Your spirit lives with me – *forever*.
I am so grateful for you.

Come Hell
or High Water

Life Lessons from Hurricane Katrina:
Facing Life's Greatest Challenges, No Matter What

Marvin LeBlanc

Table of Contents

Preface

Walk over to the sink and fill up a five-gallon bucket of water. Then lift those five gallons of water into the air. Those five gallons weigh just over 40 pounds. Now multiply that bucket in your hands by 100,000. Picture those 4 million crushing pounds of weight; those hundreds of thousands of gallons of water bearing down on your family home. That is just what happened to my wife, my daughter, and me. Those 4 million pounds of water washed away life as we had always known it.

The Katrina water attacked the landscape with unprecedented power, weight and fierce violence, taking the homes on our block, pulling all the soil out from under them, and washing them 100 feet into the highest part of the street.

In the immediate aftermath of Hurricane Katrina, my home became the most photographed home on television. Helicopters would hover vertically over the 17th Street Canal and the remnants of my home 24 hours a day. They would fly circles in the hot Louisiana sky and roll pictures of my life washing into the floodwaters.

We had been evacuated 60 miles northwest to Ascension Parish. Most of the rest of the good people who surrounded us were anxious to get back to their homes and neighborhoods. Unfortunately, my family and I knew that we didn't have to rush home. Every day at six, we were on the news. The world could see the remains of our home just as well as we could.

On Sunday morning, August 28, 2005, my home shared its property line with a drainage canal that had its own built-in levee. That drainage canal became the location of the now-infamous 17th Street Breach: ground zero of Hurricane Katrina's destructive aftermath.

My home had featured a swimming pool with an overgrowth of bamboo around it, and a giant pine tree towering over our heads, shading us from the scorching sun of hot Louisiana afternoons. It was absolutely gorgeous.

But after the storm, the entire concrete foundation of the swimming pool, the swimming pool itself, and the trees were gone. All that was left of my house was a cement slab and the vertical joints for framing. All of the bricks and sheetrock were completely washed out. There were parts of our 50-year old pine tree in what had been my living room.

Imagine looking at a two-story apartment building. Now picture a floodwater line just below the roofline. If you had been sitting in your car, in my driveway, at the time that the 17th Canal Breach had occurred, you would have had to escape, then swim eight feet upward to get to the surface of the rushing flood waters.

My wife's mother Marilyn was a music teacher—she taught piano lessons. The piano that was in the foyer was never found. The refrigerator was stuck in the top portion of the rafters because it had floated that high. The only thing we found that had stayed was my wife's treadmill. Everything else was gone.

The home next to ours didn't even exist any more. There was no frame or roof left—all that existed was where the concrete had been poured. Everything else was completely washed away. We had never seen anything like that before.

There was total darkness. No light, no birds, no sound.

People have asked me to get in front of groups because of my stories and losses. I don't know if it's because of the pain or the emotional sensitivity, but when I tell my stories, and they imagine the destruction, the tears well up in their eyes as well. They think about the heartaches and trials they have been through in their own lives.

We all either have or will have a Katrina. Our personal Katrina is a tempest that rages through our lives without warning, destroying the security and stability we often take for granted. This is a book about your life as much as it is about mine. About dealing with and overcoming adversity against all odds. I lost nearly everything in the storm, and I hope this story will help you to survive the hurricanes, large and small, in your own lives.

I have done my best to write this book with simplicity and in the rich storytelling style I grew up with. If you'd like to have a more business-like or academic discussion, give me a call. This one will be short and sweet, with pictures and stories, and a taste of Cajun country. And come on down sometime to taste the flavors and feel the warmth of New Orleans and St. Bernard Parish.

It has now been years since the storm, and the memories of that fateful day still scrape my nerves raw sometimes.

I'm so thankful for each of you across America that poured your hearts out and gave to me, my family, my team members, and my community—whatever you gave. St. Bernard Parish is still alive and well. Remember St. Bernard and remember New Orleans. We're so much more than what you see on the news. Come enjoy our city. If you come, you may never leave.

Stay in touch with this Cajun businessman, you hear?

- *Marvin LeBlanc, June 2011*

Part I

**"Time can heal and cloud a memory,
but it's your responsibility to remember
what happened in New Orleans and
make it a part of who you are."**

— Barack Obama

Chapter 1
The Storm Comes

At 8:00 a.m. on a Saturday two days before Hurricane Katrina struck the Louisiana shoreline, I was in one of the most beautiful places on earth: Manresa Jesuit Retreat House[1] nestled on the Mississippi River in Convent, Louisiana. In the 18th century, it had been a community college with huge antebellum white columns, several hundred 125-year-old oak trees, and a Spanish mission chapel built with wooden pegs.

At Manresa, you can go into a four-day silent retreat no matter what denomination you are. Their memory hook is:

Manresa – house of sacred sod,
where nobody speaks to anybody
and everybody speaks to God.

Everyone is encouraged to practice the spiritual exercises of St. Ignatius.

Before leaving for Manresa, I had cut a check for $250. The check would represent a donation for the services rendered and to maintain Manresa's beautiful facility.

I found this check over a year later. I never submitted it at the retreat. Why? Because it's a ritual that on Sunday mornings, the attendees of the retreat would receive their envelopes and then turn them in prior to the final 10:30 a.m. instruction on Sunday.

But we were not *there* that Sunday, because something unusual happened. Because of that approaching hurricane.

---

[1] *http://www.manresala.org*

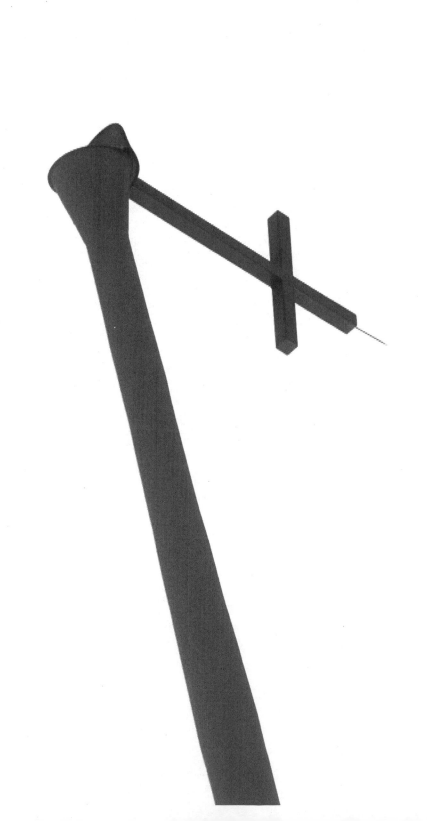

At the Saturday breakfast just past 8:00 a.m., the Jesuit priest conducting the retreat announced that we would need to gather our belongings and head home. The retreat had been cancelled because of a hurricane called Katrina.

My initial thoughts: "Well, honestly, this was kind of a pain. I went through all the trouble to get close to God. I came over here and now I'm being sent away?" It was just really confusing.

That was the last time I laughed for about 18 months.

That day, like most of south Louisiana, we thought we were going to have to evacuate for a couple of days and then everything would be fine. But everything was not going to be fine.

Just like that, in an instant, your life can change forever—without your consent and outside of your control.

From that moment at breakfast, I would have to make thousands of hard decisions that ultimately led me to where I am. And who I am.

It would prove to be my life's *defining moment*.

Before August 28th, 2005, there was a time in my life when I was materialistic. From 1991 to 1994, I had worked five or six years with the insurance company that I represent. I wanted so badly to get to the next level, so I built a house at the 18th hole of a golf course.

The Eastover Estates gated community is still recovering at the time of this writing. But not the 36 holes of golf fairways and greens. They are all grown over: a constant reminder of Katrina's hard slap in the face to a once beautifully manicured piece of property.

So I built a huge home with 16-foot ceilings and triple-crown moldings. I had lights laid into the Triple Crown that would indirectly light the ceiling.

I miss the office in my home the most. Terry, one of my customers, is a master craftsman, trimmer, and woodworker. He installed custom-designed mahogany bookshelves. My office had a big ceiling, slat-wood floors, a gorgeous fan, and three big windows with a beautiful overlook.

One particular fall in Eastover, the wooded area next to my office had an eagle's nest in it.

I had opportunity. I lived "too large" of a life in the early 1990s, but my daughter was getting older, and we wanted to position ourselves around where her high school, Mount Carmel Academy, would be. We wanted her to get acclimated to friends in that particular neighborhood.

Two years before the storm, my wife and I had sold our dream home and moved to a three-story town home. It was 6814 Bellaire Drive. The same home that would only two years later become the star of breaking news photography.

E very single year since Katrina, I don't have the words to describe the psychological devastation so many of us feel when that hurricane icon on the television makes a turn toward the Gulf of Mexico.

People from Pensacola, Mobile, Biloxi, Gulfport, Slidell, and New Orleans—all the way west to Lake Charles and the Texas border—see that icon with the same dread. It's impossible not to have your blood pressure go sky-high.

That hurricane icon represents evacuation. It represents a possible life change. You can come back after the storm, but the question is: come back to what?

When you see the hurricane symbol on the Weather Channel enter the Gulf, the first phase of your attitude is *excitement*. You're excited and interested, but you're not too worried until the hurricane icon moves closer and the weatherman shows the orange or red funnel of the area where they anticipate the hurricane is heading.

But when The Weather Channel indicates that you're included in that funnel area and you've lived in South Louisiana for a long time, you are going to enter the second phase of your attitude: *frustration*. I will break that frustration phase down into six parts on the following page.

In business and in life, I have found that we go through three phases of attitude. The first is excitement, as I mentioned on the previous page. The second is frustration, and the third is recommitment.[2]

During and after Hurricane Katrina, all of New Orleans sank deeply into the frustration phase, myself included. Here are the six sub-phases of frustration that everyone in my business and personal life were experiencing:

1. Shock
2. Denial
3. Fear
4. Anger
5. Justification
6. Acceptance

1. **Shock** is the first sub-phase of frustration. You are going to be shocked at the realization that it's possible you're going to be hit with another hurricane. Intellectually, you know good and well that the possibility exists, but when you see that icon again, you're still going to be shocked.

2. **Denial** comes next. You deny that the weatherman could possibly be correct. What are the chances we'll have another Betsy or another Katrina? This may sound humorous, but there are people who have lost everything and still believe that New Orleans and the surrounding areas will be spared in a future hurricane. I find that absolutely amazing. Never having another Category Five hurricane hitting New Orleans not only defies my logic, it defies all science.

---

[2] Inspired by *Split Second Choice: The Power of Attitude* – by James Winner.

3. **Fear** is the third sub-phase of frustration. You say, "My goodness, what if this weatherman is telling the truth? What if we really are going to stay in the funnel and get hit?"

4. **Anger** is the most important sub-phase. In Cajun terms, people get "pissed off." That's the point where they're going to have to make a critical decision. Contrary to popular thought, there are two kinds of anger: positive and negative.

Negative anger overtakes you and you submit to it. You say, "Man, we are done for. We're poor and we don't have a car, so we're going to wait it out." That is the thought of helplessness. It's the thought of irresponsibility and denial or it could be just a thought of poverty. Maybe you literally can't get out.

Then you have the old-timer attitude and say, "Nobody's going to make me move out of my house." Some distorted, possessive, hard-headed, ill-conceived reasoning. Most are just plain-old stubborn.

Positive anger is where I chose to hang out, and it's where all of the people who are coming back to New Orleans chose to hang out. It's where I'm asking *you*, the reader, to hang out when life is overwhelming and your frustration is overpowering.

Positive anger gives you the opportunity to bypass the other sub-phases of frustration. If you stay in negative anger, you're going to go straight into the fifth sub-phase.

5.   Next, you'll start trying to find a **justification** for all the reasons why it's not *your* fault that all of this is happening. You won't have a sense of ownership. Instead, you might have a sense of entitlement, thinking someone else should fix this and send a helicopter or a boat.

6.   The last sub-phase is **acceptance**, when you accept that this is your fate, which makes you then stay in a stage of being stuck.

The good news is, that if you have **positive anger**, you can avoid looking for something to get excited about. You can avoid *blaming it on others* and you can take on an *ownership* spirit.

Don't play the victim.

Don't play the blame game.

Own it!

With an ownership spirit, you can *recommit*. This is the most important, and final phase of your attitude.

Marvelous Moment

Take a few moments and write down your thoughts about the following questions, either in this book or on a separate sheet of paper.

1. How can you recommit to taking an ownership spirit, both at work and at home?
2. What is your "Hurricane Katrina"?

"We're not even dealing with dead bodies. They're just pushing them to the side."

— Former New Orleans Mayor Ray Nagin

Chapter 2

The Levees Fail

Although various scientists and others predicted that someday the levees would fail, it was mere conjecture in our minds until the day Katrina hit.

Luckily, we were able to evacuate in time, along with thousands of our friends and neighbors. Those who didn't evacuate our community had a hell-on-earth experience. My family were among the safe and secure ones, who watched on television as our entire livelihoods went up with the floodwaters.

We watched in horror as water swept away whole houses, entire blocks, and our entire parish was left in ruin. But for the first few hours, all we could think about was the people who had chosen to stay. Where were they now? Would they survive?

From the report of the U.S. Army Corps of Engineers' Interagency Performance Evaluation Task Force (IPET) comes the following eyewitness account from St. Bernard Parish:

> This eyewitness reported that power went out about 0500 on Monday morning Aug 29th 2005. She saw rainwater in the street, but no floodwater at about 0800. Sometime shortly thereafter the floodwaters came and in about 15 minutes they were up to the ceiling in the lower floor. They stayed at that level for about 10 days. The wind abated about 1600 hrs, which is approx when they could get a boat to rescue her and her husband and son. She stated that they have 10-foot ceilings in the house... The water was black in appearance.

The water in our homes and our streets was black – contaminated by a million-gallon oil spill.

S t. Bernard Parish was the only parish completely decimated by Katrina; covered over by thick, black, suffocating water.

Out of the 26,900 homes of my friends and neighbors, only a few were still habitable by the time Katrina left her mark.

Our part of Louisiana, even though it has a rich history, was sitting poised for something like this to happen. Of course, if the Corps of Engineers and others had planned better, the storm surge might not have inundated our homes, but at some point, the "big one" was coming. Scientists were just waiting for the "other shoe to drop" when a hurricane would ride right up the canals and flood New Orleans.

St. Bernard Parish is in the marshy delta of the Mississippi River. That contributes to our love of crawfish and other delicious seafood, but it also means that we were not sitting on much dry land when the hurricane came. What happened is that, in order to develop commerce on the banks of the Mississippi River in and around New Orleans, the Corp of Engineers, various oil companies and others dredged out channels that would make shipping easier. Each year, those channels grew wider and faster.

We often talk about "Mr. Go" down here – a channel that was built against the express wishes of the residents of St. Bernard Parish. It served as a conduit or funnel for the storm surge in Katrina's wake directly towards the weak and poorly maintained Industrial Canal's levees. Mr. Go and a comedy of errors made the breach and the floods happen.

Long story short, the canals, and the dissipation of our marshy swampland made Katrina the vicious attacker she became. By herself, she wouldn't have done more damage than a few downed trees and broken windows. With the help of humankind, Katrina changed the landscape forever.

As a Cajun might say, "This is an almost, *mostly* true story..."

A Yankee was lost on the beautiful, meandering south Louisiana bayou called Blind River, right by Lake Ponchartrain Basin and the Bonnet Carré Spillway. With cypress trees on every side, the Yankee pulled up to the front of Whitey Duplessis's river camp and hears the darndest moaning and groaning from Bones, Whitey's Catahoula hound dog.

The Yankee asks Whitey, "Excuse me, sir, what's wrong with your dog?"

Whitey said to him, "Well, there's nuttin' wrong with my dog. Why you ax' 'dat question?"

The Yankee asked him again. "Whitey, that dog's moaning and groaning is really bothering me. Can you *please* tell me what's wrong with that dog?"

Old Whitey leans over to the Yankee and says, "Well, to be honest wit' you, he's lyin' himself down on a sharp nail. An' you see it's hurtin' him. But it *doesn't hurt him quite enough to make him move and get up!*"

The point of the story is that, like that Catahoula hound dog, I was laying on that *sharp nail* in 2004, and didn't know it.

The irreverent storm named Katrina ravaged the area and exposed the poor choices made decades before by the Army Corps of Engineers when the levees weren't designed properly.

The reason New Orleans flooded was not Hurricane Katrina; it flooded because of a man-made disaster, because of poor engineering. Plain and simple, poor levee construction.

We were all Catahoula hounds, waiting for the storm.

Marvelous Moment

Take a few moments and write down your thoughts about the following questions, either in this book or on a separate sheet of paper.

1. How are you a "Catahoula Hound"? What kind of "nails" are you lying on?
2. Make some resolutions right now. Not at New Year's, and not the next time you think about it.

**"There were all these people
Just waiting there for someone,
But nobody came, nobody saw,
'Cause nobody wanted to go there at all."**

— Harry Connick Jr., *All These People*

Chapter 3

Up on the Roof

❧

Without a doubt the saddest part of the Katrina saga is the story of people stranded and left behind. People who crawled up into their ceilings to live for days without aid. Animals and humans all clung to anything they could grab hold of, hoping to survive the flood, only to die on the roofs with no food, water, or relief from the sun.

Dozens of levees were breached during the storm surge that came with Hurricane Katrina. Nearly 2000 people died, and hundreds of thousands were traumatized and scarred. The damage cost nearly $100 billion, and people didn't know whether the city could ever recover.

But even as New Orleans was rebuilt, and now that it is again the center of a huge rebounding tourist industry and is the pride of Louisiana,[3] we could not forget those faces in the attic. The people who were stranded in their homes.

There is a greater lesson here. No, not just the most important (and obvious one) – listen to hurricane warnings, and evacuate early! The larger lesson is that *the human soul can do amazing things*. You can do nearly anything if you put your mind to it. People and animals survived this tragedy by sheer will to live. Let's learn that lesson, and live each day as if it's that important. Because it is.

---

[3] For more on New Orleans' tourist industry, visit www.neworleanscvb.com

After Katrina, we lived with our loving, caring relatives in both Ascension & Ouachita Parish. In three different homes. Always feeling that we were imposing. Always feeling unsettled. Uncertain. Unimaginable. Unbelievable. And one day it finally dawned on me. We were *homeless!*

I cried for a solid hour. Loud! Alone in my car. And that made me feel better until the next day when feelings of despair & helplessness returned as persistently as a Louisiana mosquito on a hot, humid, sultry August night.

If you have ever explored the wonders of a beautiful state park in an *RV camper*, you know that it can be both exciting and exhilarating. But, if you're like most people, you would only want to do this for a few days. And once you've scratched your itch for the open road & you've sufficiently conquered the adventure you sought, you are excited to know that you are going back home *to your own comfortable bed.* How would you feel if you were forced to live in that camper for six months, a year, or maybe longer?

Katrina survivors had to "apply" for a FEMA trailer and go through a long, complicated process. FEMA was notorious for routinely changing out their personnel every two to four weeks, so it was always an incredible headache to get anyone to answer the phone much less provide straight answers. And every time that you would begin to make progress through the landmines of their inefficient, bureaucratic, runaround system, your *FEMA person* would be replaced. And you would have to start over and tell your entire story from the beginning again to the newly-assigned FEMA person. Even when you were lucky enough to actually *get* them on the telephone, they would rarely make a promise they would *keep*. They always needed to talk to another *third party* that was conveniently never around.

K atrina was my crossroads from mediocrity to significance.

I know that might sound strange, since it was such a difficult time in my life and in the lives of all of my neighbors, family and friends. So let me explain:

Zig Ziglar famously said that you can get multiple college degrees on your daily commute back and forth from work if you listen to books.

I've always gotten my messages from books. When I was most in despair, I would go to Ziglar's school in my car, and hope would be restored.

In searching for solace and respite from Katrina's grip in the years following the storm, after long days at the office hearing story after story about how my clients lost everything, I found refuge in books. And those books have helped me to earn my Ziglar "doctorate".

Come hell or high water, is there a way that we can evacuate from our current level of mediocrity? From poor team performance? From a poor marriage, unhealthy relationships, or obesity—which is nothing more than a lack of discipline to evacuate from the table?

Marvelous Moment

Take a few moments and write down your thoughts about the following questions, either in this book or on a separate sheet of paper.

1. Have you somehow gone, or how can you go from mediocrity to significance?
2. Have you ever felt stranded "on the roof" of your career or your life? How can you "evacuate" from there?

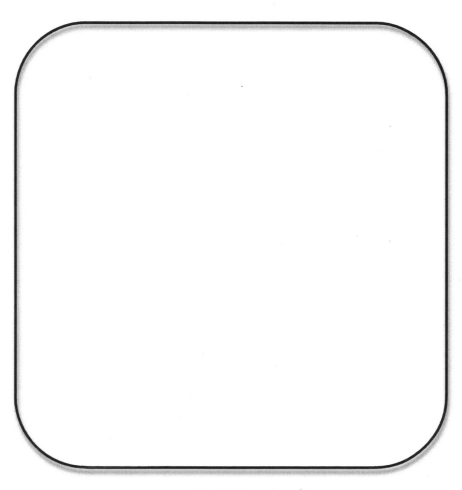

Part II

"When you come to the end of your rope, tie a knot and hang on."

— Franklin D. Roosevelt

Chapter 4

All Hell Breaks Loose

My best estimate shows that I lost as much as 68 percent of my monthly income within the first 180 days after the storm.

The reason is that a Louisiana Insurance Commissioner instructed all insurance companies to have a moratorium on sending out any bills to the disaster area. The insurance companies would honor coverage even if bills were not paid. They counted on the good faith of the citizens and policyholders and expected them to pay at a later time.

There was no mailbox to be delivered to and there was no immediately functioning post office in St. Bernard Parish. And the insurance commissioner didn't allow us to send renewal notices and bills to mailboxes that no longer existed.

My compensation agreement did not state that my income was always going to stay steady or go up from one year to the next. I was fortunate that I worked with the world's safest insurance company and they did the best they could to help me on a financial stipend until I got on my feet.

There was no manual for my company on how to handle the post-Katrina environment. Actually, they wouldn't have even been required to have to done *anything* for me. But they did take care of us, and I remain very loyal to them to this day.

Anyone who survives a hurricane is a better expert for the next one. My thinking is straightforward. If you are entrusted with the good faith of the customers who have chosen you, then you should be good enough to keep the promises you made in the event of a covered peril.

As long as you're fighting, you're not losing. We've got a lot of quitting going on in America right now.

Way too many people are saying, "Oh, the economy is so bad." Get off that! If you have an employee who says that, get rid of them.

Most of what you say to yourself and say to others is what you allow others to say to you. You don't have to be around negative people. You do not have to spend your life around people who are not going in the same direction that you are.

You have a different choice.

Low self-confidence and low self-esteem are career stealers.

It's all about the questions you ask. It's not about the answers you get.

Celebrate your failures and embrace what you learn from them.

How can an entrepreneur lose his entire team, save one and rebound to the pinnacle of achievement among his peers? Enduring the loss of an experienced team, finding jobs in other states for displaced employees to work, handling an emotionally distraught customer base – all while having no permanent office from August 2005 through June 2006. My team achieved the coveted Chairman's Circle honor from the company I represent for two consecutive years following Katrina's unwelcome visit.

How can you come back from that and make Chairman's Circle in two years? That involved losing people, rebuilding, starting over, and moving 30 miles from our original office.

Very responsibly, the insurance company I represent had made a decision to restrict the amount of homeowner's insurance we could offer. Essentially, they had said, "We talked to some weather forecasters and we believe that in the near future a Category 5 hurricane will hit and destroy New Orleans."

At the time, all I could see was that they wanted to take my opportunity away. I thought they were making up this story about a Category 5 hurricane that would hit New Orleans. We hadn't had a big hurricane hit New Orleans since Betsy in 1965.

I had begun slowly disengaging years before, but I reached my highest level of disengagement in 2004—a year before Katrina would attempt to drown our hopes and dreams. I was very bitter and thought I knew more than the company. I focused more on being a scratch golfer than on leading my team and being the example.

I read my 2007 goals for Chairman's Circle several times every day. I had them taped to my credenza and thought about them all day, every day.

I enrolled my team in an Agency Development Program (ADP). It helped us to reengage, identify the building blocks, and to focus on being there for others and making a difference in their lives. ADP was about growth, finding common ground, reassessment, and self-evaluation.

I stumbled upon tandem appointments, which helped take us to the top. There were training benefits, multiline benefits, revenue benefits, and higher value benefits. I embraced Paper Days – People Days. My lunch hour was always intentional.

Entrepreneurs and small-business people are the most important people in my city (yours too, in case you haven't thought about it). People look to you for leadership—economically and emotionally, whether it is verbalized or not. *You are always being observed.* Realize that others will model your behavior, especially if they perceive you as being in a position of power and influence. Therefore, be extremely protective of how you spend your time and who you spend it with. Live your life by appointment and schedule your appointments for your upcoming month first. Before all other appointments. Set appointments for yourself to be alone, to read, ponder and "be."

Why did I become reengaged? Because I felt needed again. It became about the customers and not about me.

I stay continually amazed at how clueless many managers are about what their team members want, yet they've been managers for years. Ask questions of your team members and listen to their responses. Your job is to make sure they have one heart.

When put in charge, take charge, and have the courage to do the right thing. Continue to show appreciation of your team. Courage is not passing it off or acting cowardly. Courage is taking the necessary action steps to get to a worthwhile goal. Make a commitment to the goal and make a commitment to get better. Taking risks is OK, too. Players who take no risks usually lose. Don't let your ego get in the way.

Leadership is essentially the ability to lead, inspire, and influence. Leadership must define the talent. Leadership and teamwork are intertwined. You are the leader of your team, so lead by example and don't expect your team to carry you. The following few easy actions can help you maximize the output from your team:

• Hire the right people (discussed below). People won't burn out if they are the right people, if they are open to training, and if you continue teaching them.

• Utilize their strengths. Maximize everyone's talents through leverage, training, expectations, accountability, consequences, and empowerment. Realize that *very rarely does the true core of a person ever change. Sadly many managers tend to manage around their team members' weaknesses. Avoid this tendency & forever strive to manage around a team members' strengths.*

• Train. Hold training sessions from 8-9 a.m., four days a week. An employee cannot find money if they don't know what they're looking for or where to look for it.

I had a great upbringing in a blue-collar family with a whole lot of love. I had compassion for other people and the clients I served; for my customers in St. Bernard. I was honored with their patronage for 17 years.

My team and I had made promises before Katrina, and at this point, our clients needed us in their lives more than ever before over those previous decades.

Clear and simple!

Deep down inside of our soul, we all have an inner voice. It's the cumulative experiences of parents, teachers, preachers, loved ones, coaches...people who instill their intangible values like courage, character and self-confidence, long before you were old enough to be able to define any of them.

I carry the voice of my teachers and leaders when I lead my own company. After Katrina, in order to get my team to really understand the depth of commitment and drive it takes to accomplish a task, I started to lead and inspire them to be relentless and never give up, *come hell or high water*. No matter what it takes.

It doesn't really matter what we need to do because we know what the goal is and we are committed to "git' 'er done!"

Build Pride in Your Company

- Make winning important: most people prefer to be on the winning team.
- Give awards to your team for top producers.
- Catch them doing things right.
- Share the detail of your company's top recognition program (such as Chairman's Circle) with your team members. Inclusion is critically important.
- Create competition with other groups.
- Use e-mail team building messages regularly.

The Five Impossibles

1. You cannot over-communicate—it's impossible.
2. You cannot listen too hard—it's impossible.
3. You cannot produce significant numbers without written goals—it's impossible.
4. You cannot motivate people—it's impossible. You can only hire motivated people.
5. You cannot have a high-powered team with low energy people—it's impossible.

Marvelous Moment

Take a few moments and write down your thoughts about the following questions, either in this book or on a separate sheet of paper.

1. How can you build pride in yourself and/or your job?
2. Are there other "Impossibles" in your life?
3. Have you had moments when all hell broke loose? What did you do?

"Life is a shipwreck but we must not forget to sing in the lifeboats."

— François-Marie Arouet (Voltaire)

Chapter 5

Coming Back to New Orleans

⚜

The first time I thought of going back was when the government issued passes. The National Guard and other authorities down in the parish monitored every access and egress. I was anxious to receive my official pass.

I went to Katrina-beaten St. Bernard Parish on September 11, 2005, which coincidentally was the fourth anniversary of 9/11. The magnitude of going back into St. Bernard exactly four years after those fateful events was overwhelming for me.

To residents of New Orleans, Katrina was our 9/11.

On September 11, 2005, I was instructed to strip buck-naked and take an ice-cold decontamination shower underneath a water tank. After leaving my *own neighborhood*.

David Dysart, a US Army colonel and commanding officer, took a leave of absence to come to St. Bernard. He had seen the destruction down here, and he told us that this, in his opinion, was worse than Fallujah.

Such was the magnitude of the hopelessness we were facing.

Thank goodness, my family's story wasn't life threatening as so many others were, and it was also not the typical survival story. I hadn't stood outside in the wind and torrential rains as some others had. But we were scarred nonetheless.

I don't believe in homeostasis. It's bullshit.

Balance is bullshit. Balance works from a lectern, but when you talk to anybody in real life, balance is bullshit.

No one great ever achieved greatness and had balance. I don't believe it.

What I'm writing here is controversial—everyone who's ever written a book on balance would disagree with me. But do this for me: close your eyes and think of the ten greatest people who have inspired you and turned your thoughts upside down (in a good way).

My bet is that most of those ten individuals were great, but they might not have been wealthy nor had more than a college degree, maybe not even a Master's degree. Where would you be if those relatively "insignificant" people hadn't been in your life? Those people were game changers for you and me both.

I recently had a chance to visit with my fourth grade teacher at one of her former students' funerals. She was 80 years old.

The student who had passed away had gotten on the bad side of some choices, and it was a sad day. But I had a chance to tell her that day what an incredible impact she had on my life. I am so grateful that I had that opportunity to tell her how I felt.

So many people don't have a chance to go back and pay back all those mostly unsung heroes who don't realize how great they were, but live on in our souls. We see their faces in our mind's eye. We know their names.

I feel we have a responsibility to the people who paid the price for us.

S hips are safer in the harbor, but they were not built for that. We are not built to merely stay in one place.

Life is so exciting. There are so many things we all still want to see and do. And all this stuff we go through in life is nothing more than us committing to different choices.

On the flip side, lots of days I don't feel like I'm getting a good hand from the dealer, but that's the hand that I have to play, so I do it with as much marvelousness as I can.

Without adversity, there is no personal growth.

Usually I try to learn from mistakes and take a lesson from hardships. But there are times when I look up at the sky and say, "Lord, I've grown *enough* today."

There is no victory in lying down.

You will win as long as you keep fighting in this great game of life.

Don't ever accept being mediocre. Be marvelous, no matter how bad things get.

I am a goal-driven, intense person. I have always showed up for work, come rain or come shine, and I live my life day-to-day and month-to-month, with one hand on my appointment book and the other on my BlackBerry (soon to be iPhone). I have never taken my job for granted, even when I am at the pinnacle of success: the company for which I work is not going to change to accommodate me when I have a head cold or a bad day. And not even if a flood takes away my home.

The point is that we still have to succeed in spite of adversity, no matter how difficult our circumstances. In fact, that's really where true character comes from.

Many people spend more time building their dream home than they do building their character. And when the "flood" hits the fan for them, they will lack the tools they need to overcome adversity. I too was once the same way. I would spend more time planning golf vacations than I would planning for our lives.

How much money is in your savings account?

How long will that last?

The average American will not make it 100 days; they're living that close to hand-to-mouth. It's not just because they're overspending. *They're under-planning.*

Imagine that some major corporation like Google, Apple or Coca-Cola were to invite me into their headquarters and ask me, "Marvin, you've been around the world, and talked with many people. You're confident enough, and you sound like you know what you're talking about... So, could you tell us what the next ten years are going to be like for our company?" That's not an easy question for anyone to be asked, let alone with my knowledge of what can happen when disaster strikes.

One thing I know is that I've seen a lot of people. I have had fantastic mentors. I've read important books. And I've lived through Katrina.

So what I'd tell them is this, "The next ten years are going to be a lot like the last ten years. Every decade is going to be mixed with opportunity and challenge.

Right now is a great time for opportunity in our country. There will also be more people who lose their job in the next decade than ever before, and there'll be more millionaires in the next decade than the decade before.

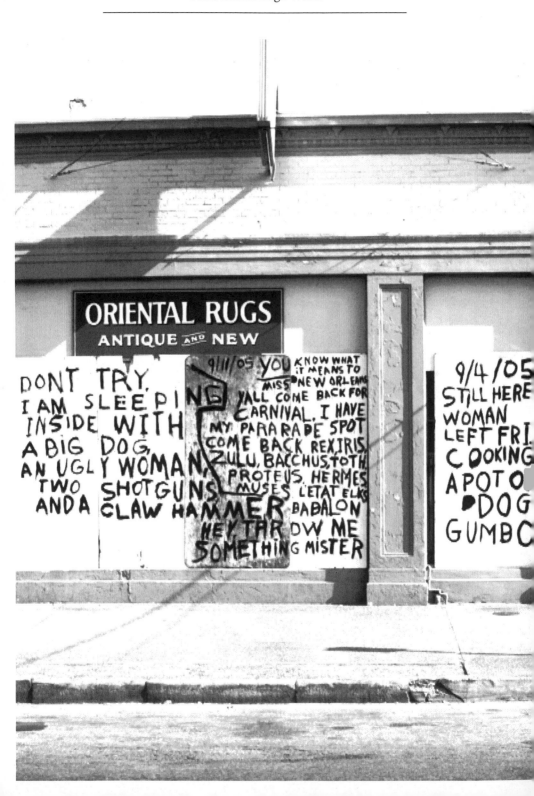

I'm a south Louisiana boy. I'm from a small village called Duplessis, in Ascension Parish. I was very influenced by coaches and teachers, and I got a full scholarship to Louisiana State University in sports medicine. The eight years I spent in Baton Rouge involved graduating from LSU, working a stint as a paramedic for Baton Rouge Ambulance, then moving on to become a Corporate Training Specialist for James L. Winner & Associates, Inc. (the local sponsor of the world-famous Dale Carnegie Training Systems).

By most people's standards, I have never really left home. I've always lived within 100 miles of my birthplace.

There are people who have lived in 10 or 12 states by the time they're 40 and they're okay with it. For me, it's hard to grasp that. I'm interested in other cultures and I won't say "never", but being a Cajun boy, I don't know if there's enough money in the world for me even to live in, say, Shreveport. North Louisiana, after all, is about as culturally different from south Louisiana as Alaska is from Florida.

I'm not that worldly, either, to be honest. Heck, I think I'd even have a hard time finding where the hell South Africa is on a map! (But I'd love to visit)

The point is, I love to experience new cultures, and although I feel like I'm open-minded, I know that, whenever I travel anywhere, I willfully come back to my *mosquitoes* and *humidity* and *gumbo* and *jambalaya*.

My roots are deep.

CC's GOURMET COFFEE HOUS

Shortly after the storm, I was in a Winn-Dixie grocery store in Jefferson Parish when a reporter from *Time* magazine tracked me down for an interview. I couldn't stop, so as I grabbed items off the shelf, she did a "walking" interview.

When the article came out, I had little recollection of meeting her because every day was jam-packed, high-intensity. I was working 18-hour days. I have never had a chance to thank her for interviewing me that day as I walked. I wish I could find her business card somewhere to thank her for caring and listening that day.

The entire nation was beginning to listen, and we needed help.

When I speak about Katrina, I end up talking about the systems that were put in place after Katrina—those processes that we did in my business daily in order, not only to get back on our feet again, but to get to Chairman's Circle, the pinnacle level of achievement for our company.

You don't get there by closing your eyes, saying in hushed tones: "I want to get to Chairman's Circle," and then finishing with: "I wish, I wish, I wish." That won't make it happen.

You have to start by saying, "*This* is the goal and *this* is what we need to do per *quarter*, per *month*, per *week*, and *this* is what we need to do per *day*." It's the only way there.

Marvelous Moment

Take a few moments and write down your thoughts about the following questions, either in this book or on a separate sheet of paper.

1. List your most important goals personally and/or in your job.
2. What are some steps you can take to reach them?

"It's important to address young people in the reopening of New Orleans. In rebuilding, let's revisit the potential of American democracy and American glory."

— Wynton Marsalis

Chapter 6

Rebuilding St. Bernard Parish

"Birds sing after a storm; why shouldn't people feel as free to delight in whatever remains to them?"

— Rose F. Kennedy

St. Bernard Parish was flooded with water from what scientists estimated was a 25-foot tidal wave.

After Katrina, there were fewer than five houses that did not take on water in the entire area. More than 99 percent of the homes in St. Bernard Parish were flooded with anywhere from zero to 13 feet of water—and that parish was mostly above sea level.

The challenge was not that St. Bernard citizens lost their homes. The challenge was that people *lost their way of life*. Right now there are less than 25,000 citizens in St. Bernard Parish. They're great, hardworking people—unbelievable craftsmen and great tradespeople.

St. Bernard has not lost its soul or its identity. But it is different now nonetheless. Let's say there used to be 12 houses on the street you lived on. Now, eight of those 12 homes are only represented by a concrete slab or a vacant lot. And only two of the remaining four homes are occupied by people you knew before the storm. The others are usually a young couple seeking the opportunity to buy real estate at a very good price. They hope St. Bernard Parish will come back in 10 or 15 years so they can capitalize on their investment.

So, of course we were concerned about losing our homes, and we were concerned that our cars were found on our roofs, but that was not the biggest problem. It was terrible that deer and other animals died at the apex of a roof because of the water level, but that's not what's really bad.

What was and is the biggest challenge is that a community had to entirely *recommit* to its future existence.

S ome people left after Katrina, and other people said, *"Come hell or high water*, I'm staying... I don't give a damn that FEMA isn't helping me. I don't care about the politics or how difficult life is. I don't care that I don't have running water. I don't even care that I don't have electricity. St. Bernard is my home and I will not leave."

Those are some hardnosed people and they'll fight like hell. Until hell freezes over. *And hell did freeze over the day the New Orleans Saints won Superbowl XXIX. WhoDat Nation Forever!!*

Those hardliners salvaged the thread of the community right after the storm. The police department, the fire department, and tons of government employees and St. Bernard Parish council members spent days on the roof of the government complex building.

There were those who had witnessed 45 to 50 people hanging onto one 17-foot boat trying to get to a safe place. Survivors were driving those boats and couldn't give you a number of how many people they saved. The water from Katrina made Hurricane Betsy (1965) pale in comparison.

Over 1800 people died in the storm and aftermath, and there was also great mental illness that followed because of the stress associated with the storm. It's unfair for all of the books to even come up with an estimate of the fatalities that happened, because the death toll continues even to this day.

It was war, just without the blood.

A person's true character was very easily exposed during that time. Some retreated and "lost it" due to the pressure and all the unknowns. Others surprised themselves by rising above the hurt, the pain, the devastation, and the uncertainty that lay ahead of us.

It was this group that somehow convinced ourselves that we were on the road to someplace better. It was our job to find that road for the benefit of all.

It didn't matter whether you were my current customer in St. Bernard Parish or not. I was more than willing to help you.

So I decided to publish my cell phone number in the newspaper. *Whew*, did my city (of 70,000 people) need answers! And they needed them *yesterday*. I probably should have thought through that decision a little bit more thoroughly.

I had made a decision, and I would stick to it. Some people run and some people face their fears. I was compelled to act.

Frankly, it was not that hard of a decision. It was based on character. You need to make character-based decisions in your life, even though sometimes you're going to have to do some things that are unpopular.

After Katrina, I became *re-engaged* and *re-committed*. Some might call it obsessed or fixated, but my desire to succeed was so intense that failure was not an option. My team met with a lot of people. We put in full days and made every day count. Our reassembled team met with hundreds of people.

Our claims partners were more than extraordinary. There's a reason the company I represent is a world-class company with worldwide name recognition. It's our people. It's our culture. It's the reason, year after year, that we are the best value for the insurance dollar. Nobody does it better. And I do mean – nobody.

Obviously, I did not have much of a personal life once I committed to helping the citizens of St. Bernard Parish. My family felt abandoned at times while I was in St. Bernard fighting with FEMA and sorting things out for our clients.

Before Katrina, I had never been involved in politics. I had never gone to a parish council meeting. I had never walked the streets campaigning for any specific candidate.

After the storm, I became a charter member of the St. Bernard Citizens Recovery Commission. It is a matter of public record that the charter members of the St. Bernard Citizens Recovery Commission received the Keys to the City and were made Honored Citizens at a later time. To the people who know me, it's hilarious how a person with my "curseful language" (as my daughter would say) could ever be considered an Honored Citizen. *Don't tell me miracles don't still happen.*

Quite simply, the original charter members of the St. Bernard Citizens Recovery Commission were hard-working citizens and business owners who loved St. Bernard Parish, and recognized that many of the "relocated" citizens needed their voices to be heard. Especially when they were still evacuated without a home to return to. At the core was our desire to have residents return safely and under favorable living conditions.

On October 5 2005, local realtor Cliff Reuther and I conducted an "Operation Recovery" meeting in the St. Bernard Parish Courthouse. The title of the meeting was "Your Goals are Our Goals" because there was some confusion as to what the St. Bernard Citizens Recovery Commission did. What was the organization's purpose? Was it a political organization? People thought it might have been a paid position and all kinds of weird stuff. I had to explain who I was and what my role was.

The "pay" was in committing to a cause when everything was uncertain. I wouldn't trade that for a pile of money.

I became "media certified". I needed the training necessary so that when radio or TV reporters wanted information, I would not create any additional controversy. The training proved to me how little I knew about the media.

My short speech was pivotal for the good will of the company I represent with the officials and citizens of St. Bernard Parish. I was passionate and committed to getting the job done.

From then on, I was the company's liaison for St. Bernard Parish and, *come hell or high water*, I was going to do whatever it took to help all St. Bernardians get down the road to someplace better. It became an obsession, but it was one I chose.

I never regretted it.

The following is the text of my speech that day:

Good morning, Commissioner Wooley, Parish President Rodriguez, all council members and distinguished guests.

It is truly great to see your familiar faces again.

I am Marvin LeBlanc, 18-year business owner and insurance agent here in St. Bernard.

My role is to keep the lines of communication open between St. Bernard officials, various authorities, and the claims process of the company I work for.

I believe that the company I work for is the greatest insurance company the world has ever seen. We stand ready to meet the challenges our people face here in St. Bernard.

And like good neighbors, we are here now—on the ground and available. We are committed to spare no expense in getting the job done quickly, fairly, and safely.

Your goals are our goals. Here are our next three goals:

1. Complete the handling of all flood claims within the next 100 days.
2. Maintain a physical presence in St. Bernard and adjust our resources as the population demands.
3. Inspect all property as soon as authorities deem it safe to do so.

T here is only one way I was able to go from Katrina to Chairman's Circle within a year. Teamwork.

Marvin's 32 Commandments of Teamwork

1. The navy seals do everything in pairs; working in tandem is critical.

2. Constantly communicate and connect all the players.

3. Differences of opinion need to be calmly and respectfully heard.

4. You can't have a high-powered team with low talent people.

5. Clarify each team member's position and have them play their position.

6. Diversity brings value, respect, and use differences to round out the team.

7. Back up others who need help. Nurture, but don't become an "enabler."

8. Is your attitude of helpfulness and willingness to jump in noticeable by all?

9. Great teams embrace great practice. Drill, rehearse, role play.

10. True professionals never stop practicing. Are we true professionals?

11. Be prepared to sacrifice for the team. It's the price you pay for membership.

12. Help newcomers make entry.

13. Play down yourself and build up others. Can you help others perform higher?

14. Self-importance is not important. Being "others-centered" and "customer-centered" is.

15. Spend time with your teammates. "Togetherness" gels a team.

16. Can you help inspire discipline into the team? Instill taking ownership of your position. Encourage self-discipline. Require self-initiative.

17. Make sure you make a difference. Are you executing your role?

18. Staying "busy" does not make a difference. You need to do what counts.

19. Effort comes down to effort – not talent.

20. Are you contributing in such a way that clearly adds value?

21. If you weren't on the team, would your value be clearly missed?

22. While great teams are fast and efficient, more importantly they do not panic.

23. Help create a climate of trust, keep your word.
    Be accountable to your commitments.

24. Good teams must be able to take criticism and coaching.
    Vital to help whole team function better.

25. Know what to do without being told and do it.
    Think for yourself.

26. Good followers lead themselves, freeing up the person
    in charge.

27. No leader is without weaknesses.

28. If your leader is authentically engaged, they will listen
    if you initiate.

29. Be a good sport. This promotes harmony and sense of
    fair play. Show respect.

30. Stay away from putting others down, finding fault, and
    promoting yourself at someone else's expense.

31. Forgive team members who foul up. You can't get fired
    for making mistakes. You can get fired if you never
    make a mistake.

32. Compromise, share the spotlight. It can't always be
    about you.

Marvelous Moment

Take a few moments and write down your thoughts about the following questions, either in this book or on a separate sheet of paper.

1. How can you work better with your team, at home and at work?
2. Which of the "commandments" are most appropriate to your team, and why?

**Don't judge each day by the harvest
you reap but by the seeds that you plant.**

— Robert Louis Stevenson

Part III

"There's nothing that cleanses your soul like getting the hell kicked out of you."

— Woody Hayes

DON'T WAIT FOR
YOUR LANDLORD
GET TO WORK ON YOUR
HOUSE. NO EXCUSES

Chapter 7

The Mirror

I went into the bathroom, looked at myself in the mirror, and I made a commitment. The day was August 30th, 2005. I made a commitment as deep in my soul as the commitment I made the day I became a father.

That commitment was this: "*Come hell or high water...*" (as you know, I was in the middle of both of them) "...I am going to be the most positive son of a bitch I can possibly be to these people who are destitute and have lost everything."

Can you imagine going back to your own home that is so devastated that there are no personal belongings to salvage? When they went back, there was no need for a Caterpillar bulldozer to come and sweep away the debris. There was no debris. Can you see that in your mind's eye? Can you feel what that would have felt like?

Carla Lee, one of our team members, found only a spatula and a CD. Everything else in her childhood home was gone forever. A surveyor had to come and put a mark on where her property began and ended. There was nothing left. Except hope.

When you wake up the next day with no hope, it's over for you—it doesn't matter whether you're 24 or 84. Life in its simplest form is just *hope* and *moving on to the next day* and *having a reason to love and live*.

I 'm not saying that I haven't had health problems in the last five years. I'm not saying that other people should have done it the way I did it.

The time after Katrina wasn't the time for me to worry about me. Basically, it was a minimum of six days—lots of weeks it was seven days—waking up at 5 a.m. and staying on the phone until midnight.

There were times when I was on the phone with one customer for four minutes, and during that time, 17 other people would call and leave messages. These calls were from friends and customers scattered all over America—even from Wyoming—who couldn't get local news and didn't know what to believe on the news. Quite frankly, a lot of the time I was telling them the same thing, but they wanted to hear it from a person they trusted. They wanted to hear me. They wanted to hear our team members.

That led our team to being *significant* and not *successful*.

I had notebooks upon notebooks where I wrote down every single phone number—and I never had a Blackberry phone until after the storm. Now my Blackberry has thousands of phone numbers in it.

After Hurricane Katrina, I have been thinking very much about dreams. My daughter's dreams, my dreams, my friends' and family's dreams.

Do you have a dream for your life? Have you given up on an important dream? Have you accomplished your dream? Do you clearly see your dream? If you don't have a clear dream, no strategy will save you.

People don't reach their dreams because they don't have valid reasons to reach their dreams. Talent without passion equals potential without possibility. If you have to constantly talk people into their dream, then you have to let them go.

Put your money where your dream is. Be willing to bet on yourself. Don't compare yourself or your dream to others. You know you own your dream when you can't be talked out of it. When you own your dream, nobody has to get you up to fulfill it.

Lead your life instead of accepting your life. Articulate your vision and stay focused. Make the right decisions and manage those decisions daily. The people who are successful are the people who handle problems.

Love what you do and do what you love.

Don't put off your dream. Do the most distasteful tasks first.

Make a sign that says, "Do not tell them what you can do—show them!"

Repeat 12 times before bed: "Tomorrow I will do everything that should be done, when it should be done, and as it should be done. I will perform the most difficult tasks first because this will destroy the habit of procrastination and develop the habit of action in its place."

Carry out these instructions with faith in their soundness and with belief that they will develop action in body and in mind, sufficient to enable you to realize your definite chief aim.

Have a vision of what you'd like in professional and personal life. Write down what you truly want and make yourself accountable. If you don't do this, you will be victimized by the ceiling of complexity.

Write and record. Don't get too caught up with the end result. Just get caught up in the process—the journey.

Stay committed to simplicity.

Identify the names of your top customers (for example: your top 20% revenue generating customers) and have them available at your fingertips in a handy notebook or appointment book. On a rotating basis, sincerely commit to seeing or talking to them on a daily basis. No, I didn't say to email them!

A lways:

- Keep harnessing your passion and sharing it with the proper people.
- Keep listening and be sincerely interested in others' thoughts.
- Stay steadfast in your authenticity and integrity.

Marvelous Moment

Take a few moments and write down your thoughts about the following questions, either in this book or on a separate sheet of paper.

1. What do authenticity and integrity mean to you?
2. What can you say into the mirror each day? And how can it help you with your goals & dreams?

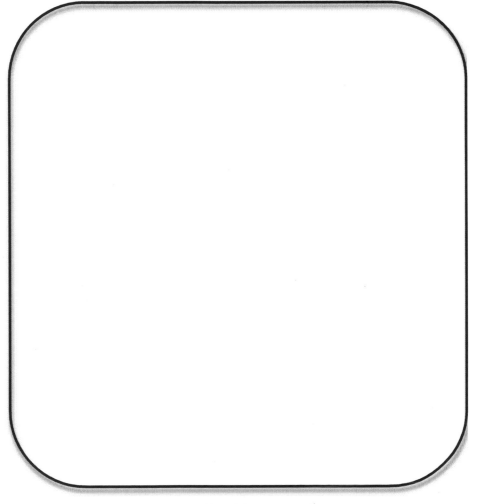

**"If we will be quiet and ready enough,
we shall find compensation in every disappointment."**

— Henry David Thoreau

Chapter 8

Marvelous Mentors

There is a God and it ain't you!

I've been going to Manresa Retreat House since I was 17. There was a Jesuit priest there—Reverend William Topmoeller—a big guy who looked like a right guard for the New Orleans Saints. He had a huge stomach, much like my grandfather, the devout Hendrick LeBlanc. Yes, his stomach, the size of a woman eight months pregnant wanting desperately to complete her last trimester. So this baldheaded guy with big, thick glasses stood up at the altar and it was all real quiet. He took a big, deep breath and he yelled at us—scared me to death—and he said, "There is a God and it ain't you!"

That was 10 or 15 years ago. I got the chills. He knew what he was doing because we probably needed to be bitch-slapped out of our state of thinking that it's all about us.

When a sales professional is thinking about his commissions before he even makes the presentation, that ain't going in the right direction. Those customers can feel it. They can't explain why they didn't buy from that sales professional, but they pick up a bad vibe—nonverbal negativity.

It's like Mama or Daddy told you—respect that gut-level feeling and move away. Buyers are the same way. They respect their natural instinct to say that something they can't explain isn't right. It's because too many people in sales don't understand what selling is about.

When I was seven years old, my parents hosted the Catholic Youth Organization (CYO) from St. Theresa Catholic Church at our house. In 1974, my mother and father won the God and Youth Award for sponsoring the CYO.

My dad would be in his rocking chair, and my mom in her recliner. Not necessarily talking. Rather, they would listen intently to teens discuss their frustrations and challenges. Countless times Dad would not get to bed until after 2:00am, only to get up at 5:30am to drive 50 miles to Georgia-Gulf Chemical Plant. Mom and Dad's selfless gift of their time has been one of the greatest gifts I was ever honored to receive.

You, too, possess the capacity to give your time and your "ear" to those that need it.

Those C.Y.O. kids (as Mom would call them) would take all the furniture and move it against the wall so they could dance. We played 45- and 33-rpm vinyl records. We'd jitterbug and listen to old music—Percy Sledge, Otis Redding, Van Morrison and Marvin Gaye and all the music of the 1970s.

In 1980, my senior year of high school, I ran for president of the diocese of Baton Rouge, which incorporated about 38 churches all around the 100 miles of Baton Rouge. I had always been in school plays and I had been in front of groups of people, but that was the first time I remember where a whole hell of a lot was riding on the quality of my campaign speeches and meeting with people. On that weekend, I spoke to a thousand kids, and I was nervous, and I loved it.

That 1980 C.Y.O. experience and my life-altering Katrina experience would ultimately lead me into the hallowed membership of the National Speakers Association[4], something that I treat as a very high honor.

At the very heart of the National Speakers Association is a core value that they have aptly named *the privilege of the platform*. And with that privilege comes the *responsibility* of the platform. We must always respect groups and companies that compensate us for our efforts. They invest in us so that we will condense our life experiences into an impactful delivery that will serve the needs of their group or organization. That level of responsibility and privilege reminds me of the core values that my parents, coaches and teachers taught me from a young age, and encourages me to follow in the footsteps of my greatest mentors.

At home, I was exposed to two very opposite ways of how to live & approach life. I certainly saw the not-so-good choices my mother made in her later years. I had also seen the choices of incurable optimism my father made. Away from home I was bathed in the compassion of teachers like Mrs. Evelyn Gauthier & the discipline of coaches like Mr. Bruce Lavigne who were instrumental game changers for me in my life

I think about their voices and faces on a daily basis to have that pay-it-forward attitude. I feel very responsible to pay it forward and I have several unpaid, unofficial mentoring relationships with some people younger than me and some who are much older than me.

---

[4] Find out more about NSA at www.nsaspeaker.org and www.nsaneworleans.com

W hen I first started thinking about my future, I was 17 years old. I was actually looking for a vehicle on a used car lot. There were probably less than 15 cars in the lot.

This is where I met Noel Landaiche. I don't know if he really saw anything in me other than a young, energetic high school student who worked at the grocery store and played high school football. Landaiche was involved with a multilevel marketing company out of Utah called Meadow Fresh Farms. He got my attention—maybe he mentioned money or appealed to my nobler motives in some way.

As fate would have it, I was invited to an introductory meeting held at an old tire warehouse building, of all places. They had set up portable chairs. Meadow Fresh Farms made powdered milk. The powdered milk had sweet dairy whey in it, and it was and is great for those lactose intolerant folks out there. Sweet dairy whey is one of the highest quality sources of protein known to man.

Yes, money was a motivator for me, but the idea of *owning* my own distributorship was even more appealing. I was *young* and *open*, so I *listened* and *got involved*. I think I actually had to lie on the distributor application because you had to be 18 to become a distributor for this marketing company. But I got involved. In 1978, I drank the product and to this day, the original product of Meadow Fresh Farms is still in my pantry.[5]

I got excited about the whole concept of selling. I didn't know what I was doing, but enthusiasm is more important than technique. Many people have knowledge and technique, but they don't have excitement and enthusiasm.

---

[5] Now produced by Wheymilk USA, LLC 1-800-737-WHEY (9439).

When I got involved in Meadow Fresh Farms, I met a person who has since passed away—Carleton Ferguson. It would be difficult to find a more eccentric and energetic man. Ferguson was a devout Mormon, a widower, and an inventor. He quoted poetry without hesitation. Books were stuffed in every nook and cranny throughout his house.

When he died, I had no knowledge that he ever had so much as a social security number. He represented himself in front of the IRS, and using their code, proved that as a US citizen, he did not have to pay taxes. I don't think he ever did.

Ferguson drove a beat-up old station wagon with wood on the side. That wagon would get around 60 miles per gallon. He was a very intelligent, articulate engineer. He had invented some type of additive for the fuel system and it generated not only power, but fuel efficiency. When I met this man, I had an opportunity to get my curiosity fueled in ways that were very impressionable at that time in my life.

In his late 70s, Ferguson could do a thousand deep-knee bends and hundreds of sit-ups and push-ups without any trouble. Inside his living room, he had a trampoline that was about three feet in diameter. Because of his belief in stimulating his lymphatic system, he would watch TV programs at night and he would bounce on that trampoline until the TV program was over.

Carleton Ferguson was a really eccentric, amazing man with a zest for life. His house was literally falling down around him. If the termites would have left, the house would have collapsed.

Books were everywhere you could imagine. This man was an expert nutritionist. He had an organic garden in his backyard and an orange tree by the side of his home. He took an interest in me. There are many people who don't believe that I'm a fantastic listener, but with Ferguson, I was intrigued and inspired. He lives inside my soul in every waking moment. His spirit and energy live inside me. I am so grateful that I had an opportunity to have this man come into my life.

Ferguson and I loaded up his station wagon on a hot July day. We left without any air-conditioning and went to Milton, Florida. I'll never forget it. We were welcomed wonderfully by a Mormon family Ferguson knew.

That summer when we were driving from one town to the next, Ferguson was showing me what it was like to be in sales and I was hanging on every word. We were always stopping at every roadside produce market because he didn't eat any processed food. We lived on raw nuts, beans, fruits, and vegetables. That was Carleton Ferguson. I'll remember him forever.

I ask salespeople, "Can you define what *sales* are? Have you ever looked up the word *sales* in the dictionary?" Never in my speaking career has anyone in my audiences responded to me with the correct root word of *sales*. We can spend our whole life working in *sales* and yet not know its origin. That astounds me. So here it is.

It comes from *sellan*, an Old English root word meaning *to give*. It doesn't mean to take, or to sell door-to-door like a charlatan. It doesn't mean to connive or to manipulate. If everybody really knew what real salesmanship was about, they would understand that real salesmanship is about real *give-manship* first. We've got so many people living in this capitalistic society who are so involved in me, me, me. Nobody really gives a shit about what *you* want until you help them with what *they* want. *Thank you to Lefty Lefton for this revelation.*

We have to answer the question of the prospective buyer: "What's in it for me?" We have to make it all about them. It's a sick, altruistic turn if you really think about it. If you satisfy them first, you're going to get enough of what you want. You're going to have to wait.

It's kind of like a good gumbo. You have to bring that gumbo up to a boil, then you have to slow it down, and you don't rush it. If you rush it, you'll burn the hell out of the bottom of the pot, and the gumbo will taste starch. You have to have a little patience. You put that gumbo on a low fire and you wait. It's like one-day-old wine. Nobody ever drinks one-day-old wine or one-day-old Jack Daniels. It's not good until later! It's the same way with sales. We have to wait. We can't be so self-consumed with paying our rent and our bills that we don't stop and ask some good questions.

Marvelous Moment

Take a few moments and write down your thoughts about the following questions, either in this book or on a separate sheet of paper.

1. How could your life/job be more like slow-cooked gumbo?
2. Describe a few of your mentors, and how they influenced and shaped you.

**"I have woven a parachute
out of everything broken."**

— William Stafford

Chapter 9

Breach Birth

I always thought I was special and different.

My mother had seven miscarriages before finding out that she was pregnant with me. So you can understand why she wasn't very happy the day she got "the news." To add fuel to the fire, on that very same day, my dad was notified that he had been drafted into the army. The year was 1961. And life was incredibly uncertain during those times.

Nine months later, on February 25th, 1962, life didn't start out well for me. Throughout my mother's pregnancy, the umbilical cord got wrapped around my neck in the womb, and a "quack chiropractor" worked hard adjusting my mom so that I could be born. And I was. Breach birth.

You would think that as hard as it was for me to get here that they would give me a great name. Wrong! They named me Marvin. Are you kidding me? Man, did I get picked on while growing up.

I've always had good self-esteem. I grew up in an extremely nurturing environment. I had an all-American mom and dad. My dad worked "shift work" at a chemical plant, but my mom never had a job outside the home. She was there every day when I came home from school.

We were middle class at best. My frame home on cinder blocks never had central heating or air conditioning. Our home was built on a dirt road, which later became a gravel road, and then one day I came home from school and was amazed to discover that we now lived on a tar road, but it never became a concrete road. And few people even know that Duplessis, Louisiana even exists on the map.

My dad made $2.18 per hour, but he worked many late nights in freezing cold or heat, working overtime because he and my mother were determined to send me to Catholic School.

Tuition was $11 per month at St. Theresa of Avila and that was big bucks in those times.

Dad always had some cars at the house and he would do body and fender work on them to make ends meet. However, we weren't one of those families who kept cars in the yard. My dad was always impeccable, and the cars were kept neatly in his double-car garage.

All business is personal. A lot of people disagree. What you're getting right now is what you're going to get. That's authenticity and transparency.

In Duplessis, Lousiana, the handshake is your word, your honor, and your character all wrapped into one. Do you know how few attorneys would be needed if this code would be more widespread?

What you always know with a person like me is that I give 110 percent effort toward the cause.

When I fail, I fail at full speed.

This attitude is what empowers me to win in the long run.

My father had a friend named Bill Davis. My father respected and adored him; he was a great chemist, and was competent and brilliant. Not only that, Bill Davis had *it*: that special quality of knowing how to treat people. And Dad respected him as the leader he was.

When Bill started a chlorine factory in Plaquemine, Louisiana, my father followed him, and they literally built the plant from the cement floor up together. And Dad later retired from there as a Chemical Superintendant. Not bad for a Depression baby – small town – no college – Cajun farm boy with nine brothers and sisters who raised themselves with their father after the early death of their mother Irene.

When my father came home from the chemical plant, he'd absolutely reek of chlorine. It would blow you out if you were in a small room with him. I could never forget that smell.

Something happened 19 years later that changed the course of the rest of my life. One summer I went to work for a construction company that was laying pipe racks in the chemical plant. The south Louisiana July and August heat was sweltering hot, and to make things worse, I was a welder's helper and I wore a long-sleeved, denim shirt with steel-toe boots, a hard hat, and a respirator around my neck in case of a chlorine leak. You also had to have eye goggles on. It was brutal.

That was one of the most important summers of my life. One day it dawned on me that sitting in an air-conditioned college classroom at 72 degrees, having to read books, and writing on a piece of paper seemed so "inspirational."

I said to myself: "Dude, you need to get your ass back in college because physical labor is definitely not what you want to do for the rest of your life." And that is what I did.

But not without some additional "detours" along the way.

In the morning when you wake up tomorrow, look in the mirror and recite what I call the *Three I Love Yous*. Say to yourself: "I love you, I love you, I *looove* you."

We're not talking about narcissistic love. What I'm trying to communicate is that *negative things are real*, and some days, the only love you're going to get is the *Three I Love Yous* when you're alone first thing in the morning.

After Katrina, I had a tool that a lot of people didn't have: the mentality to keep a consistent, healthy, and attractive attitude. The specific "Attitude Phases" *(see p. 35)* and knowing how to make the right *split-second choice* singlehandedly aided me in my effort to maintain a consistent, healthy and attractive attitude. I had to draw from that well every single day, no matter how difficult.

Come hell or high water, all you've got is you. Every day you have to start by building yourself. Your number one responsibility in your life is not your parents, children, wife, or employees. They're not your number one priority. Your priority is *you*. You cannot give to them what you do not possess inside your own basket.

Again, say to yourself: "I love you, I love you, I *looove* you." Then, say it to everyone around you. That's what life is all about.

Acknowledgments

T hank you to:

James L. Winner – Your lessons in tenacity, leadership and attitude development sustain me daily.

Mikki Williams, Certified Speaking Professional – You were the persistent stimulus that gave this project it's initial momentum.

Razz, Josh, Tina and Jenny – True, authentic friends. Your deep conversations have been as vital to me as breathing.

Lexi – It is I that have been honored to be your father figure. Keep dreaming.

Taylor – my daughter, my inspiration. Can we please not do that FEMA trailer thing again?

Georgia – my wife. For taking a chance on me over 20 years ago. Yes, it was a surprise wedding, but you could've said no. *NOT!*

Herman – my father. My first hero. You are my game changer. As you are for thousands of teens in Ascension Parish. Your positive impact on us is immeasurable.

To all of you.

I love you.

I love you!

I *looove* you!

About the Author

Marvin LeBlanc is a nationally recognized speaker and a full-blooded Cajun. He grew up in Duplessis, a small town in southern Louisiana, but his special brand of optimism has a much wider audience, and he brings his passionate presence to his "Marvelous Performance Schools" and motivational programs throughout the nation.

Voted 2010-2011 "Member of the Year" by the New Orleans Chapter of the National Speakers Association, Marvin is also the current Membership Chair for the organization, and an active speaker and trainer. He is also an 8-course Dale Carnegie graduate and certified instructor on the book *Split Second Choice: The Power of Attitude*, written by his mentor Jim Winner.

Marvin channels his positive personality and challenging experiences to empower others through his unique sharing of lessons and techniques. But he never strays far in his message from his Cajun roots. He graduated in 1986 from Louisiana State University where he earned a student-athlete scholarship, studied sports medicine, and served as athletic trainer for LSU football. He survived and thrived through Hurricane Katrina, and he still lives and works in his beloved south Louisiana.

For more information or to book Marvin for his Private Coaching, Performance Schools or Corporate Speaking Events, please visit www.MarvinLeBlanc.com

Jambalaya Recipe

Courtesy of "Uncle Herman" (My Dad)

Serves 10 hungry Cajuns

3 lbs.	**Onions**		8 lbs.	**Pork fingers**
3 tsp.	**Minced garlic**		3 Tbsp.	**Chachere's Seasoning***
1 bunch	**Shallots**		1 Tbsp.	**Black Pepper**
2 large	**Green bell peppers**		3 Tbsp.	**Worcestershire Sauce**
1 gal.	**Water**		1 Tbsp.	**Tabasco Hot Sauce**
7 c.	**Rice**		2 pinches	**Parsley**
3 lbs.	**Sausage**			

*Tony Chachere's Original Creole Seasoning

Directions:

For the Cajun Way to cook this Jambalaya grab my free directions at: www.marvinleblanc.com/recipes

Yes, I will *personally* answer all your insightful emails. Let me hear how you are using this recipe, and how you are also using the "Marvelous Moment" exercises at the end of each chapter.

Ya'll *pass a good time now, 'cher!*

Marvin
marvin@marvinleblanc.com

Resources

For discounted & bulk orders of this book:

Blooming Twig Books
1-866-389-1482 Tel.
1-866-298-7260 Fax
320 S. Boston, Suite 1026
Tulsa, OK 74103

Products available from www.MarvinLeBlanc.com:

Insurance Toolkit (2-CD set)
This collection is a surefire must-have for any insurance sales professional. Includes topics that can be applied immediately to your daily life such as vital discovery questions and a proven referral word track.

Come Hell or High Sales (2-CD set)
If you want to move your sales performance from mediocre to marvelous, this resource is for you! Includes all of Marvin's surefire strategies for prospecting, following-up, closing the sale, serving the customer like they've never been served before, and generating enthusiastic referrals for years to come. Buy a copy for each member of your team.

Katrina Revealed – Rebuilding Lives in the Big Easy (DVD)
As a photographer, Joshua Lee Nidenberg communicates through pictures. But returning to his ravaged hometown he came across music from local bands that reflected the area's post-Katrina moods. He became inspired by the compilation CD entitled Feeder Bands on the Run released by the Carrolton Station Foundation; it moved him to narrate his images with this music to tell his story of what the storm left behind.

Split Second Choice *by Jim Winner* (Book)
Our world is changing rapidly. Individuals and companies are struggling to get ahead and stay ahead. People are grappling with adversity on all fronts. Companies are fighting to stay in business. This leads to the question, "How can we cope with the changes?" or "How can we gain an advantage?" This book is about taking control of the most fundamental component of nature; our attitude. Here is your opportunity to understand these powerful concepts.

Notes